Cows in the Fog

And a Variety of Other Poems and Stories

S.T. Haggerty

Cows in the Fog, and other Poems and Stories

is available from Amazon.com books

Visit website: **www.sthaggerty.com**

Email: sthaggerty76@gmail.com

Visit Facebook: S.T. Haggerty, author

Cover Design by Kit Foster
www.KitFosterdesign.com
Drawings by John Belfontaine
www.belfontaineart.com
ISBN-13: 978-0-9860630-0-8
ISBN-10: 0986063002

With Love for Maureen, John, and Christina

In memory of my father, Richard, and mother, Virginia.

And for my brothers and sisters,
Bill, Cecilia, Chris, Dan, Dick, Jay, Joe, John, and Martha.
Someone has always been there.

Acknowledgements

Thanks to Jeff Edrich, who edited my poems, encouraged me, and helped me throughout the writing of this book

Appreciation to Linda Shaw, who copyedited the project, and Donna Christopher, my proofreader. Thanks to Vinny Dacquino, leader of the Mahopac Writers' Group.

I also wish to thank Hubbard Wells, Steve Rayl, and Charles "Junior" Bentley, who have read my stories and poems since my college days. My appreciation to H.L. Fullerton, Norm Olsen, Colin Roberts, Gwen Tibbals, Donald O'Connell, Frank Zeller, and Rich Rodrigue for their help and encouragement.

Table of Contents

Nature's Bounty

Moments

Introduction

I began my career as a published writer in my junior year of college. Since then, I have written in many forms, and found much enjoyment reading and writing poetry. Finally two years ago, I declared to myself, "I am going to write an entire book of verse."

Soon thereafter I found myself embarking on this adventure of creating *Cows in the Fog*. It all began when I decided to take a break from the novel I had been writing. I began creating some short pieces. It wasn't too long before I felt a thrill from engaging in this delightful art form of imagery, metaphor, feelings, and philosophy.

Before I knew it, I found myself with a dozen of my own poems in my hands. I began sharing them with other professional writers who encouraged me to move forward with the book.

While progressing, I reflected upon where the inspiration to write a book of poetry like *Cows in the Fog* originated. My father, a lifelong musician, worked in various positions in the music business, as a violinist, conductor, songwriter, arranger, and music editor both locally and in Boston and New York. He worked on everything from church choirs and barbershop quartets to television shows, as well as Broadway musicals.

Some of my fondest memories are of sitting in my father's rustic attic office at home as he edited music for Broadway shows. He would dip his fountain pen into an ink well and write each note painstakingly. As a boy, I was fascinated with the electric device he used to erase an occasional note. The eraser tip would spin as he touched the page, effortlessly dissolving the error. He would hand us music paper for writing stories as we relaxed in this creative ambiance. We would listen to soft, lilting music in the background, like the classic instrumental tune "Love is Blue."

Over a period of 30 years, he worked on various musical works of Richard Rodgers, beginning with the scores of an NBC program produced in the wake of World War II called *Victory At Sea*. He also edited music for Rodgers and Hammerstein's musical *Carousel* which was the personal favorite of Rodgers. It features the song "You'll Never Walk Alone."

"With hope in your heart you'll never walk alone."

I got a sense of why these lyrics were effective, as well as others on which my father edited music: "Oh What a Beautiful Morning," from *Oklahoma!* and "The Sound of Music," from the musical of the same name.

This was an excellent way to learn that a song, or poem, must convey feelings that allow the audience to make a strong connection. Only then will the bond develop.

Years later, I understood that if I were to be effective as a poet, I must successfully project feeling in my poems, whether they be about nature, recollections, or mood pieces.

Writing *pastoral* poetry made sense because I spent my entire summers in a secluded village in Vermont. My brothers, sister, and I spent hours wandering in forests, walking through brooks, valleys, and dirt roads. I felt the rhythm of the rural landscape, and experienced country life in heartfelt ways. We spent many hours in quietude, and I suppose this is where I first became comfortable listening to my thoughts and feelings.

At Southern Vermont College, I minored in English Literature, and after reading and writing in classes, I enjoyed contemplating poems, especially those of American Literature, as I walked miles down country roads.

I wrote the title poem, "Cows in the Fog," as I reminisced about these experiences. Some of my earliest memories are of chasing cows to the barn for milking at six years old. Mustering all the strength of a little boy, I managed to lift and push my first bale of hay on an old wooden wagon at eight. My brothers and I swam in ice cold brooks, and slept in haymows with flocks of bats flying overhead.

As a young adult, I also received my M.A. in journalism. In my early career, I worked as an editor for a major magazine publisher. After taking a break from the world of written words to rest my mind, I began assisting a college roommate in his business, which is called Jason the Handyman. We cleaned out basements, painted rooms, put up mailboxes and fences, and fixed other things broken around houses.

Working outside again, I experienced the beauty of nature and its subtle changes. I recall digging my first trench under a blue sky in spring. The leaves were fresh and shiny, and the scent of musk rose from the softening earth. I have a vivid memory of one winter evening when, working alone, I struggled to carry frozen green lumber so heavy it buckled my shoulders. I'll never forget the lovely, poetic snowfall that evening. It took my focus from these burdens, and I rested in the healing calm that spread over me.

I can recall painting clapboards on the second story of a home in autumn. I stood on a ladder, and colorful leaves in a chilly breeze rattled joyfully next to my ears.

The sense of relief that comes to construction workers when the days begin to warm at winter's end has always been especially heartfelt.

One day sometime after beginning my collection of poems, my daughter Christina, ten at the time, and I were hiking through the woods in autumn. We paused by a pond, and I felt a burst of inspiration that could only be expressed in the powerful simplicity of a poem. After she gave me some ideas, I needed to write immediately. My readers, or listeners, if I am reading at an event, often chose this poem, "Ponds," as one of my best. Without intending to do so, I found myself writing another poem, and then another. With the editing help and encouragement of my friends in the Mahopac, N.Y., Writers Group, I wrote Cows in the Fog.

It took me two years of immersion in poetry, studying as well as writing, to complete this book. Once again, I took many walks in the woods to become intimate with nature and to allow poetic energy to churn. With pen to paper, my first task was to observe or recall a scene or a personal experience worthy of a poem. The key was to return to a childlike state—to observe God's creations with wonder. I carefully observed trees, flowers, ponds, night skies, as well as all sorts of weather, and took careful notes in my mind. I sat quietly, far from the noise and business of life. I gave my thoughts and feelings plenty of time to give full expression. Vivid memories of my childhood on the farm in Vermont began rising from my memory. Ideas for other types of poems flowed into my mind, including humorous ones about daily living.

When people told me they "felt present," and were able to connect with the feelings I put forth in one of my poems, I found it thrilling. I write poetry to share with other people, and I enjoy reading the work of others.

***

As I added more pieces to my collection, I saw even more clearly that I needed to read and study good poetry every day. Reading other poets sets a mood that inspires me to put pen to paper. And of course, one learns valuable techniques. It takes work to understand a poem, and often I find it takes two, three, or more readings to grasp the full meaning, especially those of the classic poets. I enjoy lingering with a poem that has gained my interest until the image and meaning come into focus.

Many poets take pride in offering subtle clues, but put the onus on the reader to discover the meaning. If I was hooked after my initial reading, I would usually read the poem again to ascertain a deeper understanding. After I discovered what I believed to be the meaning, I would find myself exclaiming, "Ah hah! Got it." And I would remember that particular poem.

If I enjoy a poem, I often find myself looking up words in the dictionary, sometimes even those I recognize. Doing so can make or break the ability to grasp its meaning. Poets employ words with the utmost care. It makes sense. Not many are used.

In the past I often wondered why the great writers, like Thomas Hardy, Robert Frost, and Carl Sandburg, as well as writers today like Billy Collins, Maya Angelou, and Richard Wilbur, would spend much of their genius on poetry. Why wouldn't they write only novels, which tend to pay better and usually make a louder statement? Perhaps because one can get hooked on creating these delightful morsels, which are full of important meaning.

A world of feelings resides in a good book of poetry. As one reads a collection he will discover much about the writer's emotional journey. After all, poets often reveal intimate feelings and philosophies, as well as details about their lives. They freeze moments in time.

4

Collins, in a page, shares the feelings he experienced sitting by his father's side in a nursing home. He follows his father's line of sight, pondering about the thoughts his loved one might be thinking. Alzheimer's is taking his mind, and one can feel, with Collins, just how peculiar and poignant the situation is. Incidentally, Collins often writes story poems, which makes his work easier to remember.

Maya Angelou, in a short poem, "I Know Why the Caged Bird Sings," makes a concise, profound statement about the deep sense of frustration one feels when enslaved in any manner. She explores the contrast between the situation of a "caged bird" and a "free bird." The former "opens his throat to sing" because he is trapped. "The caged bird sings with a fearful trill of the things unknown but longed for still."

In contrast, Angelou describes the "free bird" taking off flying in the orange sun over the water. It is so beautifully descriptive. One feels "right there." Her strong images help one to easily remember this masterpiece.

Robert Frost, in the brief but powerful poem, "My November Guest," conveys to the reader his feelings of loss while walking through desolate woods. Though the trees are bare, and the birds gone, he has come to appreciate this lonely sort of landscape despite the melancholy setting. This poem's strong emotional feeling makes it memorable.

Richard Wilbur stole my attention with his poem "The Fire-Truck," which conveys splendidly the thoughts and feelings one experiences when a fire truck comes speeding through a neighborhood with its siren blaring. "Redness, brass, ladders and hats hurl past, Blurring to sheer verb."

Perhaps on the third reading, I find, for example, that I am "with" Billy Collins as he observes his father in the nursing home, or, with Maya Angelou on a riverbank as she watches the free bird fly. Or it sinks in deeper that Frost's "November Guest" is in reality his own sorrow, and he has made peace with it.

Richard Wilbur's "Fire-Truck" insisted I read it many times, and I might as well have been standing on the sidewalk of the "shocked street" for this event.

Using my experiences living the country life, my education in writing, and my employment in the field of magazine writing, I wrote *Cows in the Fog*. It is the hope of this writer that my work will allow you to wiggle with me under a barbed wire fence to chase these gentle creatures to the barn. Will you come and stand with me on a wooden plank bridge and experience a roaring white capped brook cheering a dismal valley on a November day?

Philosophize with me as I assist a young man in moving a fence busted by an apple craving bull, which already possesses more than one could ever want. As we string new fencing to widen the rogue's pasture, I ask myself if I am wrong to appease this opportunist.

Can I interest you in riding with me as I brake my car for one of those pink-headed birds called turkey vultures? This one has spent his day in an agonizing routine. In the middle of the road, he takes a bite or two from his carrion, but must scoot to the side of the road to let a car pass. Then he flaps back for more chow. I have to wonder: does this fellow have the patience of a saint or is he a glutton for punishment?

By the time I approach, he has only enough care remaining to casually lift his head, and I don't think he's going to move. Will I be able to stop my two-ton machine in time? I invite you. Come see!

S.T. Haggerty

Night Petals

Crows blend into the night
The tender furnace hums to me
Peace sprinkles points of light
Our round poem purrs on my knee,
and the sonnet petals open, finally.

The Farm

Cows in the Fog

As I drive the highway,
a thin veil of fog lingers
over the remaining patches
of this season's snow,
leaving white patterns
on beds of brown leaves,
like those on the backs
of Guernsey cows.

******

The scene takes me back
to the time I was a child of eight.
The day after school ends,
we leave our home
in a suburban neighborhood
of Victorian homes and
yards with short grass
like boys' crew cuts.
Ours is small enough that
a good whack of
the skinny yellow plastic bat
would hit the whiffle ball
over the neighbor's fence.

The car full of us arrive in Vermont,
and we stand in awe of
our summer playground,
the Green Mountains,
where acres of meadows
of tall timothy grass wave,
soon to be cut by the farmer
and baled into squares,
of which I lifted my first last year,
and muscled it up
on an old wooden hay wagon.

Our car is parked next to
the gnarly line of locust trees
with thickly ridged trunks,
like broccoli stalks with florets.
Clusters of small oblong leaves
grow only towards their tops.

We can't charge up the dirt road fast enough,
my three brothers and I,
spaced just three years apart.
Our hearts leap like flying fish.

We reach the barbed wire fence;
lift the bottom line for one another
so we don't rip our shirts,
and squirm like snakes on the grass
until all four of us stand in the barnyard.

Under an ash tree with a wide
canopy of fresh June leaves
in dull light at milking time,
a herd of cows stands huddled.

The miserable, colorless sky drizzles.
Their spirits hunched over,
the cows are still except for swishes of tails
and twitchings of their skin,
but flies merely change positions.
One or two of the gentle animals
with large brown eyes
drop their heads and give low moos.

We are eager to meet the challenge
of moving the herd into the barn
to earn a quarter pay,
and so we clap our hands and holler
until the herd finally obliges,
but I suspect their willingness
might have sprung
more from compassion than fear,

so as to allow flatlander boys to receive a smile
from master farmer Smith,
who waits below in the barn.

With choppy steps
they move down the hill,
avoiding thorny weed clumps.
A long abandoned Chevy,
sporting a high rounded hood,
holds a story I long to hear.
Rusting in the hilled background,
it is clothed in green,
like the crabapples that grow
on the trees we passed running.

Our excitement finally
moves the herd through
the barnyard, and inside,
with pure white hair,
thick as that of young men,
and a warm smile for kids,
the aging farmer,
under the flaking
white-washed ceiling,
pushes his stalls closed.
Post edges are worn to bare wood
from cows rubbing their necks,
and under my fingertips,
the wood feels waxed.

As his family has done
for over two hundred years,
he twists the blocks of wood
that lock the stalls closed for milking,
while I rest my face on the warm
side of a cow, and
run my hand over
the soft hair on the side of its belly.

I have done my job,
and the shiny quarter
clinks in the bottom
of my silver corn can.

***

I drive farther south,
and the snow patterns
on those beds of brown leaves
become fewer and fewer,
until they are no more.

The distant memory of cows
huddled under the ash tree canopy
fades out with the fog,
and I imagine it floating
through the country
until finding shelter
in a faded red barn,
and falling into a deep sleep
in the upper floor
filled with hay bales and silence,
except for the fluttering wings of swallows
landing softly on old beams.

Lonely as a Leaf

Every so often, a random
glimpse of innocence
carries me back to
that swimming hole
where the melancholy breeze
of September first blew,
the cool one that plucked
the season's first dying leaf,
leaving it to fall, lonely,
whirling to the earth.

You are whispered back to life,
brown hair matted from our swim
in the gushing mountain river
that turns the corner
through the brushy field
and arrives under the beams
of the red covered bridge,
where the knotted rope swing
threw us plunging into the eddy
just before the boulders.

Sitting on the river bank,
the short white fringe
of your cut-off jean shorts
adorned your golden thigh,
where your hand rested
next to mine, unsure.

Towels wrapped our
bare, shivering shoulders
after that season's last swim.
Your heart caressed mine.
I longed to lift your hand,
and feel your fingers
weave into mine.

After delicious lingering moments,
never having cause to expect
they would ever cease to be,
you rose, dropped your head
and tossed your locks forward,
vigorously brushing out knots
until your luscious hair shined,
and with a flip of your head,
you commanded it
back over your shoulders.

After you walked over
to the mounded dirt road
lined with dainty pebbles,
you turned and gazed
as you stood at the car door,
and the wave of your hand
punctuated season's end,
departure from the mountains.
Like the season's first dying leaf,
I was left to fall lonely,
whirling to the earth.

November

November tears the remnants
of October's robes,
stealing the forest's dignity,
perhaps as punishment
for enjoying attention from the masses
who praised their brilliance.

November whips with forceful winds,
not a whisper of compassion
for the naked tree limbs creaking and groaning,
their branches stretching to their utmost
as they try to resist cracking.

The trees absorb the shock by shaking,
but they can only watch
as their shriveled leaves,
once yellow, splashing in radiant sunlight,
scramble over barren fields.

But the trees refuse to succumb,
won't even waste time fretting.
They have no mind
to imagine toppling gales.

Autumn cold forces the life blood
of hardy perennials to retreat,
and shrivels their crowns,
but their wills are preserved
in sanctuaries beneath the soil
where they are covered
by warm white blankets of snow,
and they rest, dormant.

If only those in despair would do so.
Who can teach the ashen-faced,
who once danced in lemon light,
that the vicissitudes of November
are pushed along by sweeter winds?
Haven't they heard what we have seen?

Fence Breakers

On a blackened August evening,
the smell of fermenting fruit
coated the sticky air
as the young man searched
for a bull that busted
through the farmer's fence.

The air swished.
A presence?
He turned
and took a jolt
upon finding himself
staring into the eyes
of the rogue bull
staggering
through a grove,
intoxicated on apples,
whisky drool
running from his mouth.

A lush mountain pasture,
thirty black cows with white aprons,
and calves dancing on new legs.
Shouldn't that suffice
to content a bull?

The farmer's chore
for the young man and me:
move the fence back some yards
so as to sign over to the bull
the space where he trespassed.
Outrageous!

I had pledged
to never again
move a boundary
for a fence breaker,
opportunist of any type.

Should we not
keep the fence as set
and follow the policy
of repair and reinforce?
Otherwise, what statement
do we make?

Having told the story
of the encounter with the bull
with widened eyes,
the young man
is operating a chain saw,
sharpening locust branches
with thick-ridged hides,
most durable of native growth.
I grip one end to hold them still.

Too late to question the farmers.
Their minds are made, I'm sure;
the noisy saw spews
the fumes of my regret.

Our pliers pull the rusted staples,
we yank up the old posts,
and thirty paces back,
we sledge-hammer new locusts down
and fasten the resplendent silver wire,
careful to keep our fingers
clear of the steel scorpions.

Leaning on the sledge,
the day's work done,
I admit, though loathe to do so,
that I am again an appeaser,
but, I console myself,

"Sometimes letting go of the taken
makes one less miserable
than trying to wrestle it back."

Going home alone, the silent voices
of the farmers whisper.
"That bull has no voice like a human,
no bark like a dog,
no paws like a cat,
to plead for a door to be opened."
Can we blame him for busting fences?

The Turkey Vulture

You are a king of the sky this morning.

Gliding below the blue expanse,
your wide brown wingspan stretched,
eyes peering downward at the forest,
you circle,
poised to swoop,
but created to take only the dead or frail.

Bronze breast plump and proud,
rounded feathers edged in gold
under heaven's streaming light,
your wing tips, silver,
steer while scoping
the brush between the groves.
A mere tilt steadies your span.

Later, we meet on a country road,
You are no longer a king,
but a beggar instead,
in my lane pecking carrion,
perched upon the putrid mound;
and now your plumage appears gray,
like the sky before its end.

In a shady tunnel,
under tender branches,
innocent light pokes through,
your dark side suddenly exposed.
You are someone I thought I knew.

Begrudgingly you pull
your featherless pink head
from the hole you have pecked
in the black-striped carcass,
but you hold your place,
and defy me with black eyes.

Dining hour would have been
so much less complicated
had this raccoon exhaled
its last breath in a quiet meadow.

Life is hard enough.
Why must nature torment you,
serving your meal
in the middle of the road?

My wheels draw closer,
and I fear I will run you over.
"You wouldn't risk death for a meal.
Would you?"
Nonchalant in this pointless
game of dare, despite
my tires' crushing power,
you eyeball me,
and sparse springy hairs of white
bristle on that pink head
above your puffed breast.

What incongruity!
Is it by design or by trick of nature
that this peculiar head of yours
is suited for the shape of a turkey,
not as a crown for your noble body?

If your tiny pink head
weren't running the show,
perhaps you wouldn't be
so desperate to eat meals in the road.

But who am I to judge?
Your labor is honorable as mine.

"Move!" I holler, "Move!"
But you…you just don't care,
and now it may be too late.

I stomp on the brakes,
and my car screeches to a halt.

You reluctantly flap thrice,
and your gangly wings,
once gilded with gold
as you circled under that blue expanse,
struggle to lift you off
to the side of the road.

Your eyes follow me as I pass,
and we both know that we are all
beggar and king.

Terry Brook

I hear it roaring from the farmhouse deck,
beyond the cow barn, once red, silver worn.
It beckons me to walk down the hill to check
its pulse on this clammy November morn.

Beneath wooden planks the clear wave bold
leaps to a white cap, archs and summersaults
above smoothed rocks, turquoise, blue, gold.
The brooding mountain valley it exalts.

Most seasons its two arteries are dry.
One wider, filled by storm, rushes to feed.
The other, descending hill, stops to sigh,
but relents, and joins the streaming speed.

The brook flows through the valley undaunted
beneath the oak trees' gray skeleton hands,
and by the dying or dead, it is not haunted,
though many hang above the mounded land.

With power the brook runs its path as led.
Keeping itself from flamboyant display,
it contains all its strength in the riverbed,
surges to inspire miles, without delay.

God's Solemn Hour

Above shrunken crusted snow,
the frayed reclining sun
bounces its last shafts
off the picture frame glass
and around the somber room.
The clock thumps seconds.

The darkening mocks me
with bright memories
of you and me, and all of us,
poignant moments, revelry.

In the stillness, spindly treetops
bathe in thin red light.
Throbbing golden edging runs along
the distant, jagged tree line,
until this striking beauty fades too,
allowing the thickened darkness
that teaches me rest from thoughts.

This is God's solemn hour of reflection.
I would not summon revelry.

Two Comets, We

Somewhere in southern Connecticut
we were chattering in my car
about newly awakened faith,
when our emotions flared,
and we steered into
a sweetened bliss.

We departed the material,
transforming into comets,
and now viewing us from a distance,
I can see we were nothing less
than two spirits minus bodies
speeding beyond the cars.

Time accelerated
and we transcended the pain
that anchors humans to time.

I recall nothing of that trip
until touching down
and seeing the uprights and cables
of that grandest of bridges
that crosses the mighty Hudson,
and it was way, way down below us.

I would have been anxious
if wonder hadn't transcended fear.

Ponds: A Poem for Christina

To my daughter, ponds are a delight!

When water is freezing, smash
When heat is scorching, splash
In autumn, a canvas of colors to view
In spring, skunk cabbage shines green, but p.u!

Will

This one flutters unharmed,
merely tickled by the howling tempest.

It drills up through concrete from beneath,
Finds the weakness in asphalt, pokes through.

Squeezes between curbs and sunken steel storm drains
Roots itself in barren fields of sand
Waits without fret for leaves in a tree bend to decay
Survives in crawl spaces sealed off from light and rain.

Yank between the flowers, rising sun 'til stars
It may reappear next week,
but will lie in wait a century if need be.

It rides the wind, drops in gutters, sprouts in muck.

And one day,
a philanthropic breeze sweeps a fertile field,
and woven heads of timothy rise
and sway like freedom flags,
smiling at those who attempted to root them out.

Who? Tell me who, has the will of grass?

Long Story Short

I see him in town periodically.
This man has quite the gift of gab, you see.
To listen to him robs all of my strength,
and trees wither, he rambles for such length.

One day he spotted me, and I feared.
As he followed me in the deli, he declared,
"I will make a long story short."
I could not help but think, "What a good sport!"

He did indeed edit this tale well.
I could not help think his company swell.
Oh, but the rascal crammed in five more,
and I? I hightailed for the exit door!

A Country Memoir

Chasing Trout

Dear John,

Do you remember as kids in Vermont how badly we wanted to catch those speckled trout in the brook? We first tried baiting our hooks with earthworms, but never once caught a fish on a pole.

Every so often, you would jamb the net under a rock, and one of those dark olive speckled fish with the orange belly would be flapping in the white strings. Then we learned that was illegal. But you were not going to give up. You even talked about catching those fish, which shot under the water like missiles, with your hands. Wishful thinking. I had heard Abraham Lincoln had actually achieved that feat, but thought it was probably an old tale.

The disappointment of returning home with an empty bucket after each excursion was made even worse by the fact that we had grown accustomed to catching fish in piles. Flounder, smelt, even eels off the ocean pier at Ford's Landing in Old Greenwich, Conn., where we went to school.

In Vermont we spent many days wandering through the brook and the mountain and valley behind our house. Within a couple of hours after we arrived home on the last day of school, we all piled into the car. Mom and Dad would have the station wagon already packed and were waiting for us kids. We'd make the three-and-one-half hour trip up Route 22 until we reached our place just over the New York line in southern Vermont. From then until after Labor Day, we remained there, which gave us plenty of time to explore.

Each morning we would sit in front of that little black and white TV. I would eat two buttered slices of that ultra-soft Sunbeam bread, and you would enjoy four. The walls were covered with that antiquated simple cow-in-the-fields wallpaper, which had to have been over 50 years old. We could tune in one fuzzy channel from Schenectady, N.Y. Just to make the screen clear enough, we had to position those two silver antennae, affectionately known as rabbit ears, and removed our fingers ever so gently so it wouldn't scissor.

Old time celebrities, just as they do today, cracked the dumbest one-liners in their booths on the *Hollywood Squares* show. But their silly quips and wisecracks about current events made us laugh: Gypsy Rose Lee, Charles Nelson Reilly, and Charlie Weaver.

Then *The Rifleman,* the honorable sheriff who always got his man, would come on. (Reruns can still be found on stations today.) Chuck Connors was tall and sinewy, and feared by even the most hardened outlaws. In the middle of an action scene, that screen would burst into white and gray shockwaves. It was devoid of compassion, even for excited boys glued to the set watching the rifleman take down another criminal foolish enough to challenge him.

With the hands of surgeons, we would move that antenna left and right, but often, we could not revive our show. How were we supposed to occupy ourselves? Often the chances of persuading our parents to take us out were slim to none.

You had to travel five miles on the winding dirt road to reach the first asphalt, and that was only the start of the journey. And usually, when Mom did agree to drive us, we would first have to complete some chore like hanging all the family's clothes on the line. It was like a clothing store of shirts, pants and socks. We were a family of nine.

What were we to do if she would not take us into town? It wouldn't be time to start walking up the hill to the dairy farm for evening milking until five o'clock. So we would dig worms, and take poles down to the brook. My memory insists that we landed zilch. Catching one of those slick shiny trout that shot from under rock formations was as hard as catching a bat with a bucket. But not all would be lost. There were always toads and snakes in the fields, and in the brook, crayfish, and other creatures. After we waded through the water a good distance, we'd arrive at that man-made pond excavated by our neighbors. It was full of tadpoles, which we would watch grow into frogs. At least the pond was good for something; swimming was so icky because once you jumped in, and your feet hit the bottom, the water became clouded with mud.

The year might as well have been 1820 when we walked that valley.

There were but a few signs of the modern era, only a few small, contemporary A-frame homes. Essentially, we beheld the same Green Mountains and grazing meadows as those of many generations earlier.

Many of the barns built by our predecessors remained standing in our part of the valley, though their use had been reduced. Many were merely used for storage of equipment at this point, or for hay bales. Their middles sagged, and the vertical siding was cracked and worn. One would notice where, over the generations, they had been repaired with wood patches.

Silos with silver domes, once stuffed with shredded-corn silage, still rose towards the sky. In our own barn we would find farming antiques left there by past generations.

Remember those old hay-cutting scythes we found? Though they were probably laying there for a hundred years, it was as if they had been placed there the day before. We would take them out in the field and became adept at using them. We would hold the handle on the end, and with our other hand, the knob in the middle. We would swing them to mow the tall timothy grass with the curved blade.

Many of the simple, cozy historic farm houses stood next to hay or corn fields, and were built close to the same dirt roads colonialists once traveled.

Our road was lined with those tall haunting locust trees with the crooked branches. Their hard wood was cut for fence posts, which lined both meadows and hillsides. Holding barbed wire, often rusted to black, each post had been persuaded into its own unique posture by the frost heaves of many winters. Dried up, wrinkled "No Hunting or Fishing, Posted and Patrolled" signs were stapled to the wooden square boards nailed to the trees. As kids, they were quite intimidating. We believed someone might actually shoot us for trespassing.

Once the television picture was gone, we'd leave our 1720 farmhouse, "camp" we called it before the renovation, for long spells to climb the mountains and walk through the fields of high grass. They would be mowed but once a year, and this was necessary to keep brush from getting unruly.

The valley was silent except for that meditative gurgling of Terry Brook, about 10 feet wide in most spots. Occasionally a passing car would leave a wake of road dust, and we always looked carefully to see if we could decipher who it was. Any person was special because to see someone pass was rare, often infrequently as every couple of hours.

On some of the chillier summer nights, the men would come down from their farm on the hill to sit by the woodstove with our parents. I always felt cozy in bed upstairs, when the feelings of their friendly chats would waft up through the floor grate.

We might rise from our beds when we were little kids to go sit on the laps of the farmers or our parents by the fire, claiming we couldn't sleep. In reality, we wanted to hear the farmers talk about those who once lived in specific houses on our road, as well as take in the yarns they spun. We would want to know more.

Who hung the man in the tree down the road many years ago? They found the body swinging in the morning. There was that real estate agent who tragically choked to death on a chunk of steak. He was the man who brokered our house. What was he like?

Hard to believe there were those times when the raccoons actually walked in the doorway and we fed them scraps.

Remember that friendly old man, who had taken refuge in our valley after being in World War I? He would be walking down the road in combat fatigues, and Dad would stop the car. The man would lean in the window, and talk about the rainfall excitedly. "There's plenty of water. Plenty of water," he'd exclaim, and so we, as children would echo to each other, "Plenty of water." His black dog, which accompanied him on his daily eight mile hike, would be wagging its tail.

Then there was our farmer friend, who many years ago was engaged to be married as a young man. The story goes that his sisters chased his bride away because they needed him-- without her--to work the farm. Though it seemed to us this heartbreaking event had taken place in those "olden days," we felt sorry for him. Our parents told us he was required to begin milking cows when he was three years old.

We would walk through the village graveyard, with solemn hearts, and study the names of other hardworking families who had lived and died there over the past few centuries. Hurds, Skidmores, Bentleys. Was it in that cemetery we encountered that haunting gravestone? "I was once like you are now, and one day you will be like me."

At the highest point of the cemetery hill, that girl who summered next door to us was laid to rest. Who can forget hearing she died tragically of tetanus at age 17 after she lost her toe in a lawnmower accident.

At one time, when small farms flourished, we would have seen scores of children clapping their hands to move cows as we did. There had been a dozen schoolhouses in the 19th century, but by our time, none survived, except a couple of one-room buildings preserved as museums. As the profit margin began shrinking for small dairy farms, the owners began to close their barns, and most of the next generations sought other careers.

During the school year, the town began bussing all children to the next town around 1950, when the federal government instituted its law requiring indoor plumbing in all schools.

These stories hovered over the valley by day giving plenty to ponder. During those times, it was rare to see a soul in either direction over our long meadow to houses in the distance. It was as if that part of the valley and the mountains belonged to us.

Down the hill from our house, we would first stand on the old wood plank bridge to catch glimpses of those elusive trout that sometimes swam under it. Personally, I had no faith we would catch one on a line and hook. Taking in the ambiance of the country and the translucent water spilling over the rocks was sufficient for me.

We would lie down at the edge of Terry Brook and, thirsty or not, lap up the pure mountain tonic like dogs. Lingering in the air would be the fragrance of sweet grass and the fresh mint we would pick for Mom's tea on our way home. That brook water was so cold that our feet, in old pairs of sneakers, would ache.

We would journey down the riverbed, covered with rocks of all shapes and sizes, quartz, grays, blues, greens, blacks, brown, flat for skimming, large for damming, and boulders for sitting on. Our feet would become comfortable as soon as they grew accustomed to the water a few minutes later. We would walk long distances on the riverbed, again, always on the alert to catch flashes of the dark green brook trout. They would shoot out from under that ridge of tree roots jutting over the bank or from spaces in the neatly piled wall, built of flat rocks, under our little wood plank bridge.

Often I'd be walking in a blissful state of oblivion, intoxicated by the fresh air, sunshine, and greenery. Occasionally, you would call me out of my trances when you spotted one of those trout or snatched a frog from the shore.

I would be philosophizing, daydreaming, or contemplating those stories told by the farmers beside the woodstove at night. I might be rehearsing the words I was going to use to straighten out someone who had perturbed me. Or maybe I was wondering what it would be like to dig so deep that I would bust a shovel blade through the bottom of the earth. Wouldn't a Chinese boy be wide-eyed when he caught a glimpse of me? I might also have been trying to understand why that person we knew drank too much and looked so melancholy. At that time I had no idea others shared the same problem, and that answers were available.

But you were perpetually alert, pointing out all sorts of creatures in the distance, on the ground or in the air. I might never have noticed turkey vultures, called "chicken hawks" by the farmer, circling our coop in the air. I recall being concerned that they would swoop down from the sky, lift one of our white Leghorn chickens, and fly off. Sometimes you would spot animals, like deer, standing in a clearing halfway up some mountain. Walking in the woods, you never forgot your way back.

I might never have cared for slithering animals, but when you'd snatch one from the grass, you would behold it like it was the most remarkable thing God ever created. Eventually you won me over. Green snakes, garter snakes, milk snakes.

We'd catch them for pets and keep them in those snake cages the old carpenter from Finland built for us from wood and screening. Remember, how, as he drank cans of Schlitz beer, he told us stories. He had worked as a carpenter at the White House some time around the 1930s. His housekeeper had been a telephone operator at the president's residence also, so they said.

But the most remarkable event took place one day when the brook had carried my mind far away. I was forming a tiny pool on the side of the brook where it was low and level. My hand was a bulldozer bucket clawing small rocks and dumping them to form walls. As I worked, I imagined my building to be a real one, grand in size, a fortress on a lake.

As usual, I was vaguely aware of you somewhere ahead of me. You would have been taking in that wide perspective of the brook and valley.

I caught up as you were strolling down the brook to that picturesque bend at the foot of the mountain where the huge evergreen lay fallen in the water. That was an enchanting place, its water darkened by shade trees rooted in the cliff. We sometimes lay down in the chilly water, up to our waists. Once our heads were under, we would scramble out.

A short distance further, the water dropped to perhaps a foot or two deep. I didn't want you to get too far ahead, so I left behind my castle. I remember approaching; and you turned, gazed back at me, and lifted your hand. "Shhh," you whispered. "Shhh."

You set your gaze down on the water and leaned over. Your hand moved ever so slowly downward to the water like a knife. I then realized what you were about to do. You had not given up. You spread your thumb and index finger, and shot your hand into the water. Your elbow shook. When you lifted your hand from the water, you grinned. You were gripping one of those speckled dark green missiles with an orange belly in your hand! "I mesmerized it," you explained, your grin having grown into a huge smile.

I believe I was more surprised than the trout flapping in your hand.

Love, S.T.

Nature's
Bounty

Through a New Portal

I can picture her as a preschooler
making her way through our yard
to pick dandelions and bluebells
on Mother's Day, and soon I am lifting her
into my arms, but she wiggles away,
and will tolerate it no more.

At ten, she is walking across
the parking lot to the dollar store,
suddenly pulling her hand free,
giving me a glance
with furrowed eyebrows,
as if she is wondering why
we had ever held hands at all.

Now she refuses bedtime readings,
will even lock her door at times,
and these are bittersweet moments,
but I understand.

She is emerging like a tender leaf,
pushing away its protective red shell,
unfolding, demanding space.

Divinity affirms her,
wills this coming forth,
this blossoming.

She has stepped through a new portal,
and feels her way
through the enchanting dawn,
halting with each step
to fan away the mist
with her hands.
She peeks into her new world.
Changed.

I feel her aura in the roadside collage
of early spring, that blends tender pastels
under the light blue sky of the robin's egg.
A million dots of pale olive green.

She is sensitive like the pink cherry blossom,
the white star of the dogwood flower,
the mauve magnolia cup of spirit,
spicily fragrant like lavender lilac cones.

A miniature maple tree, red leaves sunlit.

Choir Girls in Pink

The pink morning light
shines on the mountain ranges
frosted with fresh snow.
Today is Valentines Day.

The trees appear like
a choir of little girls
shoulder to shoulder
in opaque robes,
beaming smiles of innocence
as they await their note
from the choir director.

Brightest Stars

I have granted a vacation to
the lurking fears
that live in the shadows,
haunting our daily lives.

My feet crunch gravel
as I stroll in front of
the few lighted houses
on this forest road
in the mountain valley
just after midnight,
where those we knew once dwelled.

They are the ones I imagine,
and perhaps always will,
sitting before these televisions
that cast flashing blue light through windows,
though they have moved on.

As I leave lights behind,
entering the long stretch of darkened road,
sounds of night are amplified,
and the flowing brook brushes its stones
at the bottom of the treed cliff,
the same cadence as sheeting rain.

I am spooked by an owl
piercing the silence;

"Whoo whoo whoo,"

and feel a twinge of fear
imagining a beast leaping
from the shadows.

But gazing upward, the stars gleam
against a canvas of black.

These, like compassionate loved ones,
shine most bright at the peak of night,

and cheer me like the lights
of a thousand surging fireflies.

The Gospel of Forsythia

Bearing nature's gospel, forsythia arrives first.
Triumphantly. Unapologetic for running ahead.
Like Paul announcing freedom at Galatia,
shouts in brilliant yellow, "Spring is coming!"

On the heels of the springy branched shrub,
the weeping willow's shoots, hanging
like a gentle woman's hair, suddenly turn olive.
The lady has been discreet in changing.

One unfazed family wears fast colors four seasons.
Evergreens wait patiently as screens of red buds
appear on the gray bare bones of other species,
and finally pop into crisp green foliage.
In new apparel, the forest shouts, "Spring is here!"

First Ears

With my duties laid aside
near New York City,
I weave my car through
this old snaking highway
that leads to Vermont,
and could not be more thrilled
as I climb and descend mountains,
gliding through once vital communities
where countless herds of cows
once traipsed the fields,
and traffic even stopped
for these casually striding beasts
crossing from pasture over the highway
to be milked in bright red barns,
many of which are gray and sagging now,
their stave silos built of metal rods
and wooden hoops begging silver paint.

A friend calls this 150-mile stretch,
from The City over New York State to Vermont,
"the road that time has forgotten,"
and this description is accurate,
but I do not find the ambiance
of these vacant barns
and empty pastures depressing
because the fields are vibrant and green;
the farmhouses historic and charming,
as if they are taking a break
after a couple hundred years of toil,
ready to be called into service,
so truthfully, I feel privileged,
having been given time alone here
to marinate in lifelong memories.

These ruins keep alive the story of a people,
and a way of life that has all but vanished.
Most all the families that owned these dairies
have sold off their herds,
because working their farmland
no longer brings profit enough to sustain.

I am fortunate to be headed to a farm still working,
where silver barns still stand straight,
having been nursed along for two centuries;
many of its tractors and equipment,
bailers, rakes, and tethers,
date to the 1950s, but the steel perseveres.

The farmers will have a chore for me
when I arrive, but I don't know what it will be.
Doesn't matter, as long as I am connecting
new memories to the old.

Over the years my time on the farm has been spent
shoveling manure from the gutters in the barn,
loading wagons of fresh-cut hay;
carrying pails of warm milk
and pouring it into the cooler tank,
all the while encouraged by the farmer
who would tell me boldly,
"Never say I can't."

Some of the small delights have been
dishing out grain for hungry cows,
pouring slop in troughs for pigs
that snort and squeal in delight
as the gruel runs off their faces;
cradling newborn barn cats,
sleeping in forts of hay bales,
and drinking water ladled
out from buckets in hot hay fields.

Last visit I helped to return tables borrowed
from neighbors for a community ox roast,
and in recent times, I've helped
install a cupola with a bucket lift
and nailed siding on a barn.

I pass more ruins and virtually the only sign
of industry is the thick fields
of tall cornstalks topped with tassels,
which line many stretches of highway.

Who would disagree that raising animals
and growing vegetables in fields
is the best-rounded way to live,
and anyway, how did the dairy industry
come to fade away and find itself in ruins,
here in some of the loveliest,
most fertile fields of the world?
The large has gobbled up the small.

Many of these barns built by craftsmen in
the last two and a half centuries
show increasing decay with each trip;
more cracks in the gray siding appear,
roofs sag lower as rafters weaken.
Given the extent of the wear and tear,
I'm surprised so many still cling to life.
Perhaps their stories want to be told;
maybe they cling to the belief that one day
they will again be filled at milking time.
And maybe they will.

Two hours to the north of Manhattan,
I slow for a lingering view of a barn
that has been in decline for decades.

The sun burned the shingles to brittle,
and winds tore off handfuls of them each year;
today its skin is bare and splotched with brown.
Time has crushed both ends, and the middle sags
like an old horse ridden too long.
Overgrowth is climbing its walls,
and young trees have poked
the glass from its sashes.

I slow my car to observe another barn,
which weather has pounded for decades.
I recall my urges to holler from the car,
"Put a roof on it."
as if anyone would have heard.

Reroofed this friend never was,
and what remained on top
was eaten by the elements
and licked clean by the winds;
its remains are just a skeleton
of rounded steel ribs that form the rafters,
and under those, the barn's sides sag,
so I don't think it will be long
before some force of nature
pushes the whole sad thing over.

After these two and a half hours of reminiscing,
philosophizing, and beholding country scenes,
I am at peace, my irritations dissolved,
and I arrive in Vermont where the farmers tell me
they would like me to help unload a wagon
and get bales of hay up into the loft.

Before we tackle this chore,
I'm told to hop in the truck.

The farmer puts the machine in four-wheel,
and we climb a steep mountain,
in the truck, its bed filled with hay bales
to feed the bull and his cows.

I open the truck door,
and the black farm dog,
which will growl and snap at me
if she senses timidity,
jumps out and runs through the field.
Walking behind the truck,
I tear off slices
and toss them on the ground.
Soon there is a line of hay,
and the cows hustle toward us.

***

I am taken back to when I was a teenager,
a "city boy" from Connecticut,
and the love for the farm
coursed through my veins.
Thrilled to be outside breathing
the scents of sweet grass, cows,
and the faint smell of manure
as we threw stalks of corn
from the back of the pickup truck
on August and September afternoons.

***

I am 15 and sitting on the
tailgate of an old green pickup,
flipping black bangs out of my eyes,
and tapping my sneakers on the pavement
as it runs past my feet.
Perhaps I am tempting fate.

Straight from the hayfield
with red scratches on my arms
from throwing bales onto
creaking antique wagons,
the farmer, my brothers, and I
ride across the concrete bridge
over the narrow Green River,
which carves its way
down through the valley.
Translucent ribbons of water
move over its colorful bed of stones.

Final days of summer are bittersweet,
as the air has begun to cool;
we have started making fires
in the woodstove at night now.

School will start next week;
we will return to our home
to our suburban neighborhood,
and I will wish I was not
missing the harvest in Vermont.
These are two separate worlds we live in,
and they do not embrace each other,
except for an occasional friend
from home who makes a trip to visit.
Which is truly my home, suburbia or the farm?
I often think it would be nice
for those of both worlds to mix.

The farmer slows the truck
so we can turn onto a dirt driveway
that runs along the Green River,
and we park in the corridor
between the water
and the dense field
of stalks topped with tassels
which stand over our heads,
and hold this year's first ears.

"Let's go boys," he calls out
and we push off the tailgate,
springing to our eager feet
and hurrying to the cornfield
that stretches far and wide.
"No dubbin' around," he shouts.

The wiry farmer swings a machete
with a fluid motion
refined by the years,
and chops September's stalks,
which we toss like spears
into the bed of the pickup,
empty, except for a few bale-of-hay strings.

The rough green husks
brush the skin of my hands,
and before long, the old green pickup
is piled high as the sides,
with stalks, ears, and tassels.

He drives along the dirt road
until stopping at a small area
designated for sweet corn,
a more tender variety for humans,
and slices off ears, tosses them into a burlap sack,
and says, "For your family."

We pull out back onto the main road,
driving to the cow pasture,
where I spring off the tailgate once again
to untwist the wire that holds
the rusty steel gate to a post,
and we drag it across the old logging road,
where grass has grown on the middle hump.

The cows have cropped the meadow,
except where they have
avoided thistle plants,
the inedible bones of pastures.

Upon seeing the load of treats,
the cows hustle toward us
as fast as any creature,
with full udders,
their black and white heads bobbing.

As the truck crawls through the pasture,
we throw off a few stalks at a time,
creating a long trail that will
allow each a place at the table.
One could fear the large creatures
as they amble toward the truck,
but for me that feeling has vanished
because I have learned that
they are typically gentle,
and far too preoccupied with eating.

They clamp the fat, green-wrapped ears
with their mouths, lift them,
and shake them free of stalks
before crushing them with their teeth
and chewing them in circular motions

Back in school in Connecticut,
at dinner time when I was 15,
I would daydream about the cows
while I was enjoying sweet corn,
often wishing we were in Vermont.

***

But as an adult now,
I open the door; the black dog leaps in,
up on the seat next to me.

We descend the mountain in low gear,
having unloaded all the hay
from the back of the truck.

At the barn, I climb onto
the wagon with wooden side racks,
and drop bales onto the same escalator
we used when I was a teenager
and fed first ears from the pickup.
The machine's small pedals
are attached to its vibrating chain,
and they carry bales upward on the escalator,
now rusted deep orange-black
and others take them by the strings,
and toss them back into the hayloft.

Intruders

A bare arm thrusts through the open sash.
Hands pour bread from a wrinkled brown bag,
and hunks and crumbs tumble to the asphalt.

From surrounding yards darting robins
fold their wings as they drop to the ground.
They peck. Gulp. Like maniacs,
as if this bread will be their last.
Why the frenzy, songbirds?

A band of crows lays the question to rest,
touching down in the center of the ring,
flapping their slick black wings
to keep from tipping over.
They wobble.

The more humble birds backpedal to appease the intruders,
dressed in black from head to toe.
The helpless surrender to the self-appointed,
and with not so much a sign of protest,
they accept humiliation.

Greed nearly collapsing their legs,
the crows devour good portions
with razor-sharp beaks.
Skewering a hunk with talons,
each lifts off in succession
to find the corner of a rooftop
where he will dine at a table all his own.

The robins hop three steps forward,
and look left, right,
before advancing to leftover crumbs.
They peck. Gulp. Fearfully. Madly
The gang may reappear to swipe it all.

Not requiring portions of the greedy,
each robin hops into flight,
satisfied to be cheering the world with song.

Vigilance

With its yellow beak,
the robin pecks fresh grass,
runs a stretch on blurred feet,
and chirps a series of sweet notes.
A lovely sight for me to behold,
but how is life for this beloved bird?

She halts and stands erect
between shadows of trembling branches,
and with posture like a soldier,
she jerks her head left, then right,
perpetually vigilant.

Her head turns; our eyes meet.
She pushes out her proud amber banner,
tucked tail feathers dust the grass,
her gray suit exquisitely tailored.

She must know lurking creatures long
to carry her off between their jaws,
yet no fear can be detected
in the little black beads of her eyes.

The robin seems to fully accept her humble size,
and were I to do so too, my fears would shrink.

Blurred feet run the next stretch,
and she takes more glances left and right,
until taking off from a greened slope
into a flight that defines grace.

Fluttering wings brush the air
She soars. Swoops. Lands.
Pecks the grass some more.

She turns, and our eyes meet again.
I am certain this bird is unfazed
by the possibility of unmet needs,
and I feel this message so directly in her presence
that she might as well be speaking to me,
"There is no reason to be afraid of anything."

The robin seems to be certain
that it is the creation of eternity,
everlastingly vigilant.

Vantage Points

I make my way from the farmhouse
down the dirt road,
swept with summer dust,
sprinkled with pebbles,
and walk over the tire-polished
planks of the old bridge,
stretching over the brook.

I have bathed here,
drank at its banks,
fished for its trout,
and set dams to raise it.

I take a high step
up on the mountain
where the machine blade
cut into the foot
to accommodate a wider road
when I was a boy.

Passing felled trees,
and pushing over rotted trunks,
I pull myself up inclines
by grabbing on to saplings
and welcoming branches.

Yellow stripes on trees
Stretches of stone walls
A small concrete obelisk
Old friends, these markers.

Having achieved height enough,
I sit with my back against a boulder,
gray and wrinkled like elephant hide,
with jagged edges that match
that of the one next to it,

and I suspect they broke
from one another ages ago,
but it appears as if recently.

In a silence that is complete,
I reconcile thoughts
that have occupied my mind
on so many hurried days.

Electronic voices tell me
to shoulder the
fear, guilt, and responsibility
in the wilderness of the world.

But I dismiss them because I have learned;
my hands are capable, but small,
and I search for vantage points
to make sense of my place.

I doze, and silly that when rising,
I can't recall from where I came,
and so I meander and come upon a cottage,
where a sign posted on a tree warns,
"Beware of animal traps."
I can only conclude that the owner,
by painting such an expression,
would consider me a varmint.

I wishfully walk a gully
that leads to nowhere,
but a red rooftop down towards the valley
calls for me to come.
I must go; I have no other marker.

With small steps down the steep terrain,
I once again grasp saplings and branches
to steady my feet, which hold to the earth,

but several of those unsettling issues revisit,
refusing to be cast away until resolved.

It occurs to me,
if I am to make sense of them,
I must surrender my thoughts
that I may get a glimpse
of eternity's vantage point,
the spire of truth. Christ.

Winding Brambles

The bright sun warms my face
and arms, and it heats out
from my bones
the deep chill of winter's
overstay like a hot bath.

I am ready to dance.
Strange that in all this warmth,
nature stands perfectly still.

I am anxious and,
She stands so close,
but will not waltz,
and won't say why.

Perhaps she sees herself as only
these mere sticks, stalks, and grass
in their hues of brown and gray,
but the greening is approaching,
and I envision her more as one
that clothes these stark naked trees
with tender leaves bursting from red buds
that unfold like parachutes,
excited to play in breezes.

At treetops I do detect
an eagerness in the trees to step out.
Palms tilted upwards,
with long, knuckled fingers spread,
they soak in the energy
that will heat away her chill
so she can dress her best and sway.

Is she showing polite restraint,
giving the last two patches of snow
ample time to exit the stage?
I have no way of being sure.

One, no larger than a white shirt,
laying in a roadside gully,
must be the last to melt from a pile
made high by a passing plow.

The other lies shrinking under
gracious evergreen arms,
which seem to regret helplessness.

I have no way to understand why,
at this time, this place, and this hour,
God appointed these two
to be the sole survivors
in the roadsides and forests here.

But lingering too long on
the "whys" of her refusal,
or of what has passed,
as well as what has remained,
will diminish this unfolding spring.

Left to flourish, such questions
are brambles winding around trees,
and would confuse this lovely day
like unruly, prickly overgrowth.

Friend and Foe

You frighten me by pouring,
pounding, licking, and seeping.
You delight me by showering,
caressing, and quenching.

After you storm, I relax
in the cooled air of your wake.
I have learned to love you
and to weather you.

You both frighten and delight me,
Sometimes simultaneously.

Water, you are my friend and foe.

Moments

Dappled Windows

We are hundreds
in this school of fish
of many colors,
swimming over the highway
beneath the blackened underbellies
of whale clouds cruising.

The bellies burst; rain pounds my hood,
and spatters off my windshield
as the storm attacks the earth
with such force I pull off the road.

My wipers thud furiously,
and I am relieved to silence them.
I open the window a crack,
and the faint smell of asphalt
rises with the steam
of rain meeting the hot road.

Enclosed in a cozy gray veil,
I am hidden from the world by
resting inside the tempest.

Fat drops dapple my windows,
and I wipe the fog from inside the glass
to watch rainwater flooding puddles,
and gushing down mounds.

Nature sways under the attack,
and the landscape blurs
like an impressionist painting
that invites me to sit
and take it in for awhile.

Too soon the downpour is over;
I watch the whale clouds,
with underbellies turned silver,
move along and lead me
back to realism.

Shimmering Silver

Sometimes in a moment of despair,
mustering an earnest prayer
brings forth rays of hope
that cut through the dusk
like beams illuminating
the effervescence of a wave,
lighting it to shimmering silver.

God Cried With Us

Why would the sun
wait in the wings,
instead of appearing
for one as loved as you
this day as you
were laid to rest?

It must be that God
decided to cry with us.
Gentle warm tears
fell from the white sky
and sprinkled us
as we made our way
under the tent
over your grave.

The season's first
green blades peeked
above brown stubble.
The soldier stood between
two somber gray gravestones
in the distance.
Each note of Taps
stopped in mid-air,
saluted, and lingered,
before floating away.

The last few wisps
of cold snow were melting.

You are no longer searching for,
or running from,
love as we humans do,
but rather, radiating
in that golden glow that
I imagine may be like
the soft early evening
sunlight of summer
that warms us evenly,
and you feel like you
could stand in it forever.

We can't see you, dear friend
because we are separated
by a window fogged
like the softened ice
on the pond today.

If we could, I am assured
we would see you blissfully
strolling down a gold-paved road.

In memory of John Poirier.

Send Me Soft, Silent Snow

Peering through the pane,
tainted white caps the sky,
and I would welcome rain
to wring the atmosphere dry,
but it won't fall today. I sigh.

A shroud drapes my shoulders,
and sinking into my easy chair,
the fire in my belly smolders.
Neither happiness nor despair,
this cloth of heaviness I can bear.

Not even a whispered word,
autumn's feathers have faded;
the spinning gold now mustard,
and the hills, dull have been shaded.
No matter, the fuss had left me jaded.

Ready to tumble to the ground,
the crimson has turned muddy gray,
while orange has been stained to brown,
and in a fortnight, they will fall away,
but woods endure the barren day.

70

This boredom I once spurned
lurked behind as I skipped along,
but now I sit with it as I learned.
No need to chase the happy song,
for vibrancy can't be pinned for long.

My force this slump dissolves
but it is not an hour to grieve,
for stowed away are my resolves;
it is no surrender, merely reprieve,
and this cocoon rested I will leave.

I pray, Lord, prevail,
allow no stormy foe,
divert the icy gale,
for your dale sleeps below.
Send me soft, silent snow.

White Blanket

The bottom of our front door
pushes the piled snow,
forming an angel's wing
on the porch floor.

Ice flecks in the white
glisten in the bright sun.
The blanket draping our yards
smooths over mounds, dips, driveways,
lessens the distance,
from our door to yours.

Steady Boots

My boots are born
in the storms of labor,
stitched together
with knowing hands,
leather-burnished
from sweat and sun.

Into these boots,
I push my feet,
tighten laces
around eyelets,
wrap around hooks,
and double knot
to hold them fast
against the fiery ground.

My feet are snug,
secure for the journey,
and the boots speak to me.
"Don't let us come undone,
and we'll escort you through this day
at a pace set by your heart."

I stride towards where I must go,
but the rhythm is broken
by sanitation men in my path,
as if some force
is trying to convert me
to their frenzied pace.

They leap off their truck,
charge to piles of black trash bags,
grab 'em, drag 'em,
toss 'em in the compactor,
crushing them like the mouth
of a great white shark;

remnants of rubbish
fall from the sides of its jaws
like scraps of juicy prey.

The truck lurches onward with a roar,
belching gray smoke, gasping for breath,
as a man runs, leaps back on his perch,
and clutches the iron bar.
The boots steady me once again,
and I resume my stride as
the sanitation truck turns the corner.

I walk into a deli for coffee.
More crazy vibes.
I overhear a man
whose clumps of hair
point every which way,
like grass hacked with a machete.
"I can install that toilet in two seconds." He says.

I think, "You crazy man, go to it!"

Before I've even arrived on the job,
I've been besieged
by sanitation workers rushing
and a maniac installer of toilets!

How well I know more awaits,
and so I scoop mortar with a trowel,
and build a barricade of brick in my mind
to seal out the madness.

Finally, I arrive to toil,
and a drama overshadows my tranquility.
I jockey for a place to root myself.

A guy named Speedy
might as well be hollering "Charge!"
He works frantically
carrying concrete block,
as if he's running downhill
and his brakes have failed.

"Let's attack it!
Knock it out!
Bust it out!"

How many times after watching
one of his frenzies
have I looked into the eyes
of ruin the next day?

All right, I've done it too
but not today, not in these boots.
Just as I've reset my pace,
another man named Slow 'n Stop
tramps towards us like slow drying concrete.

"Oh man, I don't feel like doing anything today,"
he says with a sagging face
and drags a bucket of water for mixing.

I stand where the trickling stream
meets whitewater,
Speedy's heart leaps like a spring.
"We can finish it today!"
But I see work enough for two days,
in this stack of blocks and bags of mortar.

I wonder why Speedy
is doomed to rushing,
as if a poltergeist,
is nipping his shoulders.

Speedy scoops up Slow 'n Stop's mortar
with a trowel, butters blocks,
stacks them one on another,
and scurries back for the next.
How is it that the people
who start with the most energy
wind up with the least?

I take the counsel of the marathoners
jogging from the starting line,
the riders of endurance horses,
taking short steps up rocky hills,
and authors of epics
writing thoughtfully.
Only a fool sprints out of the gate.

I unlace my boots and knot them again.

Slow 'n Stop announces,
"Taking a break."
Speedy sez, "I don't stop for coffee, don't take lunch!"

Slow 'n Stop sounds annoyed,
"Why don't cha take it easy?"
thinks Speedy's making him look bad.
The barricade in my mind has served me well
and kept their craziness out.

Slow 'n Stop says,
"I'm not getting paid
enough to knock it out."

The door of nightfall
closes on this day,
and the dulling sky sounds the bell,
finding Speedy fatigued;
the frenzy has cost him two hours
for piling blocks too high
where the windows will go.

Slow 'n Stop is floating
in a bog of grogginess
so unsavory that I'd like to ask,
"Is there anything worthwhile
to do at work but work?"

I am pleased with myself this day,
for I have kept my laces tight
in time with the rhythm
that fits the hands and feet of men

I have kept my feet snug in these boots
born in the storms of labor,
and double knotted to hold them fast
against the fiery ground.

Lord, keep me in these steady boots.

Mailboxes

When we lived on the long rural hill,
I came home one day to find our mailbox
lying on the ground like a dead soldier.

I'd seen him scraping hilly shoulders,
so I knew it was the plowman who wiped it out.
A town worker made a half-hearted repair,
mounting the post on a spiked metal base, but
it tipped when the earth softened.

What would complaining solve?
And I should understand;
I knew mailboxes begged for trouble,
having once ridden shotgun with a plowman.

We risked our lives
charging across blind intersections,
praying no one would smash us
as we bathed in the fumes of diesel,
plowing condo parking lots,
and we wrenched our necks
lurching from forward to reverse.

Any aspirations of plowing froze then,
and should it be my sole opportunity one day,
I'd only take a run
of a straight 50 miles to,
and 50 miles home.

Have you observed strategies for placing mailboxes?
The naïve take the path of least resistance,
and erect a new post where the former fell,
believing themselves immune from second strikes.

Realists do what it takes to prevent more pain.
My former landlord set his box
on a stack of cinderblocks,
and this man was more proud of his strategy
than he was of his diplomaed wall.

When the plow did indeed strike twice one winter,
he leapt from his chair and out the door,
but no, not to discharge anger, but thrilled
at the opportunity to display his ingenuity;
he reset those blocks one on the other,
crowning them with the mailbox like an ecstatic child.

Where practicality can trump elegance,
I've seen pipes standing behind snow banks
that bend and reach out like long arms
holding their cherished one high over the road.

But the man who desires eternal peace of mind
concretes his into a stone pillar niche
that taunts any would-be pillager, "Try it."

Our mailbox is one no plow can strike
because it stands behind a guardrail,
but we experienced a different problem entirely one night
when kids silently bashed it with a baseball bat.

Come Sunday

I find a reprieve in a small uncomplicated place,
the apartment of a friend,
a sanctuary from demands, discussions, opinions.
Simple talk is all will be.

At a square breakfast nook table,
he jabs our steak with a fork,
to tenderize the meat.

He asks, "How are your wife and kids?"
"Good," I reply.

He pours a brown glaze over the meat,
a spicy silence as a breeze blows off life's dust.

"Can I come Sunday," he asks.
"To your house for an eye round and those roast potatoes?"

"I have to ask my wife."

He forks the steak on the back deck grill.
With no expectations except to be simple,
life has slowed down,
and a rich stretch of silence ensues;
feeling flows back into numbness,
and I can see a pontoon boat
superimposed over the lawn,
meandering down a remote southern river.

No arduous long sentences
demanding to be heard,
and no cracking of the egg of politics,
just the warmth of friendship,

"You drain the gas from your mower?"
He turns the steak, now sizzling.
"Yep," I fib, so as not to be hassled;

He is a mechanic.
"Weed whacker?"

"Yep." Another tale. Wish I had.
Forty dollars to have the gelled gas additive
removed from the carburetor.

A long stretch of wordless meaningful time ensues.

Back to the ample square table,
some poignant 60s music
haunts me with harmonizing.

We eat steak, baked potatoes and large salads.

"How's your car?"
"Running good," I say.
"How many miles?"
"One fifty."

After ice cream, I doze off in his recliner.
Awakening to the dark of night, I am at ease,
realizing that there will be time
to drive home and sleep between now and daybreak.

As I step towards the door, he asks,
"You think I'd be able to come Sunday for that eye round?"

"Come Sunday.
Yes, you come Sunday."

Freedom

Off today.
I
am
alone.
The green of our lawn
and the deep pachysandra
on the hillside soothe me.

Freedom.

The stillness whispers,
"Hold my hand.
Feel your feet on the earth.
Step with its rhythm.

Behold the neighborhood
you only experience
rushing through in a car.
Meditate on its sounds,
birds, mowers, flowing brook.

Calm washes
over my brain
and dissolves the tension.

My mind begins
sorting out issues,
allowing some to vanish,
marking others "not urgent,"
and I find faith to meet the rest.

Freedom.

The sun caresses my face,
blue adorns the sky,
crisp air is T-shirt warm.

I rake old leaves and sticks
and stuff them in a barrel.

The first woodpecker strikes.
A plane engine hums above.

I drain gas from our snow blower,
pour fresh fuel into the lawn mower.
Weed-wacker gassed as well,
and it actually starts and runs!

Slowly I drive to the barber,
who cuts my hair in the village,
and I feel lighter, freer still.

I encourage myself,
to maintain this rhythm,
knowing I will forget
at times during future days,
but I will remind myself
to enter into this freedom
by allowing peace to
wash my mind once again.

Fanning Fantasy's Flames

Are you some father's disgruntled son
unable to refrain from flinging
misguided payback in our faces
because we happen to be
the ones with you now?

Are you fanning flames of fantasy,
desperate to believe
that stories of your feats
fueled with manic energy
will be etched on the horizon,
grand displays for the world
to behold for eternity?

We remain bystanders,
knowing to comment
would make no difference,
and so, we stand powerless
as fires surge across fuses
to ignite new explosions.

None of us have your grandiose ambitions, your energy.
Are you fanning flames of fantasy?
Will it be wreckage or record books?

Don't Say A Word!

My eyes peruse the vegetable garden
at the home of a friend,
where I have been pulling weeds
crowding string beans,
tomato plants, and bell peppers.

As I rub the moist, hot dirt
to make the garden floor smooth,
I observe with satisfaction
plants now free to flourish
since I have untangled them
from pointless growth.

Sweat drenches my neck
as I rise and dust off dirt,
except what has been ground
into my knees below my short pants remains.

The house guest of my friend appears,
and hands me a perspiring glass
of Perrier wrapped in a napkin.
A frayed wedge of lemon rests on ice cubes.
The cold water quenches a thirst
forged in 100-degree heat,
with blazing sun beating on my back.

Her bright blue eyes are intense, excited, inspired,
and her brilliant red blouse reveals cleavage.
In a bun, her hair is neatly wound
above the soft, fair skin of her face,
glistening with moisturizer.

Refreshed, I return to pulling weeds
as she disappears through French doors,
only to return shortly with a hoe.

With fast, frantic motions this way and that,
she loosens weeds but hacks plants too,
and I am unsettled as I observe her working,
as if some abuser from the past
has returned and is now invisible,
standing behind her hollering.

She vanishes again, but reappears soon,
this time presenting herself in a black blouse
with a neckline plunging still lower,
but her face, now drooping,
is blotched with red.
Her once vibrant eyes are dull,
and the corners of her mouth
have turned down into a pout.

She now appears to be subdued,
and I suspect I know why.
I quench my thirst with another Perrier
as she slathers me with slurred, sappy compliments,
"You are a good man. Wonderful!
I truly mean it, a really good man.
A really wonderful man."

I am saddened to see her withering.

Her friend flings his French doors open wide,
bursts through them,
and walks close to where she stands
by the tomato plants,
which I have tied to bamboo stakes,
and from my position on my knees,
I peek up to observe these two.

His face is sullen,
and scolding her as if she were an unruly child,
he says, "That's getting to be enough.
Come inside, and I mean now!"

He steps between me and the garden,
and this tall man tailgates
the petite woman with his belly,
driving her into the house.
Through the screen door,
I hear rounds of nasty insults
rifling from her mouth,
and I consider I may have to take cover
should she go berserk.

Moments later, an eerie silence falls over the house.

After I have had my fill of weeding,
I open the French doors and walk inside,
fearful that the tiniest comment could
shatter the icy silence and ignite a firestorm,

Inside I whisper ever so cautiously
to my friend, "Where is she? She okay?"

He points his finger at a closed bedroom door,
and clearly annoyed, he whispers,
"She's in there. Sleeping it off."

"How much did she drink?" I ask.
"Doesn't take her much."
"Will she remember?"
"I don't think she will."
Grave concern weights his eyes.

Then he turns his head,
and looks at me square.
His eyes peer into mine; his stare is stern.
"If she comes out, don't say a word!
Just don't say a word."

Jest

Good Grief

I welcome you, Sir. I am Gerry Bee,
human resources for this company.
We must discuss all those days out.
Your reasons are good, I have no doubt.

Yours has been a life of trauma for years,
so you must have cried a river of tears.
There are so many on your list of dear departed.
Those three fell on Ev'rest; that's how it started.

Most deaths unrelated; no one catastrophe.
A horrible streak of luck; God help is our plea.
Those aunts and seven uncles passed on too.
The firm has joined in grieving beside you.

Your three ole grannies, and those three gramps gone,
And two lovely aunts, the sisters both Dawn.
I have heard of siblings having first names the same.
With sons, the boxer Foreman played that game.

I'm told one died on a plane, another a cruise.
Two singing in chorus, two of the blues.
The heart attacks, snapped bungees, crashing cars.
Two creamed by asteroids, kissing under stars.

Just let me offer this for those you love,
be cautious on Sunday; pray to God above,
for the grim reaper takes yours that day,
and it's Friday morns you follow hearses away.

You, working amid such grief? Plain unjust!
We are letting you go, we feel we must,
so this paper explains your termination,
severance, and a planned vacation of fun.

You will have yourself a jolly good time,
Commencing with a Mount Everest climb.
And if you come down, you will not be bored
with...

...unlimited jumps on a bungee cord!

Falling Flat

Merry moods can spring from jest,
but sarcasm is not always the best,
so if that thrilling humor falls flat,
you may be considered a mere gnat.

A new fellow may not be on your page,
and he may scowl, even fly into a rage,
so do remember the lurking danger
of throwing sarcasm at a stranger.

If you can't resist the ole wisecrack,
and an acquaintance is taken aback,
smile; tell him he's an endearing chap.
Say "I'm kidding," to bridge the gap.

Josiah! Josiah! Who is This Guy Binx?

This letter is in regards to one Jar Jar Binx.
Some people love Caspar, some the great Sphinx,
but regardless of what any person thinks,
you Josiah, have a great liking for Binx.

What is it about this guy that makes him so cool?
You have great taste; i'm sure he's no fool.
Is he short or tall? Can he double flip in a pool?
Does he eat grass or beef? Or just plain gruel?

Is Binx scaly or hairy, what kind of face?
and is he gentle or rough, crude, or with grace?
Does he fly, jump or walk a fast pace?
Is he a lazy soul, or is his life one big race?

I am curious about this Binx guy,
so let's watch *Star Wars*—we must try.
T'would be a shame to let the chance go by.
When can we watch this movie? Please reply.

Love,

Uncle S.T.

Lost Your Mind?

Don't you think it's dreadfully unkind
to tell yourself, "I'm losing my mind?"
You forget an important date, a name,
can't recall that TV woman of fame?

You cannot find the keys you set down,
missed that appointment downtown.
Parked in the store lot, can't find the car,
forgot to make soup for Christmas Bazaar.

Spaced out the birthday of a loved one,
left the stove on, the roast was done.
Forgot milk from the grocery store,
but bring unneeded items galore.

Sometimes too much to get done,
and at work, constantly on the run.
The house must be kept in good repair,
ready, if your in-laws should come there.

Before you let panic ruin a good day,
listen closely to what I'm about to say.
Your mind is not lost; don't fret one bit,
because… you…have merely misplaced it.

Bookseller Vanity

Surprised was this greenhorn when he learned,
the antique book he was peddling would be spurned.
The purchaser insisted neither blemish nor tear;
all he could see in mine was excessive wear.

Vanity applies not only to humans but to books,
and so the antiquer buys almost solely on looks.
He insists on flawless jackets completely in tact,
will entertain only those with a gymnast's back.

A scribble may mark your dear treasured friend,
which a former owner graciously agreed to lend.
Can books share their stories on shelves hidden away?
I say allow them to circulate, come what may.

The seller noted my friend showed worn extremities,
but come on mister, this is called character. Please!
Who wants a sheltered book with pages pure white?
Mine has sojourned near and far, warming many a night.

Million Dollar Santa

Wire rimmed glasses.
A puffy white beard
covers his chubby cheeks.
A round paunch to boot,
but there is no red get-up
for this city's Santa Claus
between eight o'one and four twenty-nine.

In the cube of his little white fuel-efficient car,
the Santa man spots vulnerable prey
and pulls alongside.
Fearlessly (or so it appears),
he slaps tickets under wipers,
hopes in his ride, and slides on to the next.
He is no respecter of persons.

He bellows "Ho Ho Ho" to the city
but to me it translates "Watch out!"

By the time you see this ticketeer
typing at your car,
it's too late.
Your ticket has been expeditiously logged
in a little well-connected box
that cannot regurgitate.
It relieves him to tell you
there's no hope in pleading,
and he's only doing as commanded.

Fifty tickets a day
Sixty five each
Over three hundred days
You figure it out.

Each morning, I squint and scan the streets,
alert as a soldier assessing the terrain.

No parking Tuesday sign on the pole
No parking Friday sign on the steel stem across the street
No parking Thursday, street below
(I cut the vines hiding this sign.)
On another street, the faded letters are undecipherable
Two streets over, No Parking 2 a.m. to 4 a.m.
Do they actually get up?
I give hydrants double the distance.

Every so often I hustle to my car, hoping,
but that vulgar slip will be lying under my wiper
Sixty-five dollars? Sixty-five!
Worse than a wasp sting.

The city mocks me. "Ho ho ho!"

The million dollar Santa
is not there to absorb my pain,
and I'm actually glad he's gone
in his white cube
because I am spared the opportunity
to speak boomerang words.

The Transition

Two Animators, These

Too many kindred had passed of late,
and the life of my mother
would soon join those memories.

On a weekend trip to our summer house,
poignant recollections lingered
below the eighteenth century hand-hewn beams
graced by the evenly-spaced,
gentle hatchet marks crafted
by men swinging in a rhythm.

She breathed oxygen through a clear hose
fed from a hissing steel cylinder
that stood boldly in a corner
on top of the sixteen-inch caramel floor planks.
Painful to watch her suffer,
struggling to catch her breath.

So many memories of my childhood
floated in the country air.
My mother and father,
and a house full of brothers and a sister.
Friends dropping by; no need to call then.
Swimming, baseball, feeding cows.
Long hikes through meadows, up mountains.

Lying awake in the same room
where children just like us
even well before the American Revolution,
had slept feeling cozy and protected
in the cracked plaster bedroom.
Recalling one evening
when we feared a bat that
flew into a hole in the wall
and our father reached in,
came away with a bat in his hand,
and asked us why we were afraid.

Parents and farmers telling those old stories
as they nestled around the woodstove fire.
I, upstairs breathing in those tales
as they wafted up through
the ancient round floor grate.

Lying on the bank of the brook, lapping water like deer,
wading in water so cold it numbed our feet,
watching glimpses of those brook trout
darting from one bank to the other,
and leaving us to play a guessing game.
Under what rock is that fish hidden?

Just over the dirt road hill, the farmer,
in the twilight of his career,
strapping a homemade stool
to his waist by a leather belt,
so he could sit comfortably milking
as the enchanting dusk broke.

Watching him, through the wavy antique glass
of our living room window panes,
mowing a hill so steep on his green tractor
that I feared he would tumble sideways.

Watching his usually playful hired man turn angry
when duty required him to chase a freshened cow in the
forest, cancelling his plans to court a woman that night.

Local Vermont kids and us Connecticut boys,
sniffing each other's shoulders like dogs
Could we form a pack together
or would we growl and nip?

Teenage years, yearning to meet vivacious girls
on the bank of the river under the red covered bridge.
The sting of that cool fresh water forced up our noses
when we defied the rules and jumped from the roof.

A rock hits the water and it splashes every which way,
and so it was with friends coloring those years.

No grand gathering that weekend;
just the two of us.
Not a person to let emptiness overcome,
I would need to find the strength inside myself
to will away the noise of that hissing tank,
because there would be no other source of happiness.

Or so I believed.
With a knock on the door, two small boys appeared.
Bats, balls, gloves, eager eyes, lively youthful spirits.
"Uncle, we need you to come play baseball with us."
And so I stepped out into the spacious sun drenched yard
and ran towards the outfield to chase a pop-up.

Two animators, these.

Wit and Wisdom

Quips and Quotes

It will work out, and if it doesn't work out, it will work out.

***

Go into a quiet room and lock the door, or find a lonely spot in the forest. Listen to your most sincere feelings and to the Creator. They are road signs that show you the way on the journey to finding yourself.

***

Fiction and poetry writers take the excess passions produced by daily living that are otherwise wasted, and recycle them into art.

***

Because of questionable eccentricities, we call people "characters." Occasionally I run into a person from the past who had earned this designation. I am pleasantly surprised when I notice that he is cleaned up and curiously endearing. He has become a "character with character."

***

I once complained to an elderly man about someone who had talked behind my back. "In my youth," he explained, "I worried what people said about me. At fifty, I didn't care. At my age, I wish people *were* talking about me.

***

One day when I was agonizing over how to conquer a perplexing problem quickly, an old sage put a gentle hand on my shoulder. "Don't try to make all your problems disappear too fast. For each one you solve, you will get two new ones."

Nero fiddled while Rome burned. What else would you expect him to do?

***

The habitual liar is like a man who cuts each branch below as he climbs a tall tree. When he reaches the top, he hugs the tree and trembles as it sways in the wind. "How will I ever get down from here?"

***

Framed on gym and office walls, as well as pinned to college dorm walls, you see these inspirational posters of lads climbing frosted mountain peaks. Captions read, "You can do anything you set your mind to." Some guy takes "anything" literally and freezes to death trying to climb Mount Everest.

***

On Thanksgiving Day, let the turkey be the turkey.

***

A young man was describing his boss, who operates his firm in a zany fashion. "Do you think there is a method to his madness?" The guy, looking haggard, asked.
It occurred to me to say, "Sounds like there's madness to his method."

***

In college, I was inspired by a course called "Motivational Theory." We studied various techniques scientifically proven to heighten morale and business productivity. How eager I was to put this into practice! After starting my own small construction business, I made every effort to motivate lackluster employees. How quickly I learned that the best way to motivate people is to hire those who are self-motivated.

Maybe you shouldn't be dismayed if you will not be able to retire early. A number of folks who are sitting idly report that this can be harder than swinging a pickaxe in the saltiest of mines.

***

The next time you sigh at a guy who is contorting himself as he shuffles and moves paperwork strewn on the passenger seat of his car, consider this: how would you like to have your work laid out nicely on your office chairs only to have to move it from front to back as people come and go?

***

If I ever run for public office, I'll be a one-issue candidate. I will author and aggressively promote a bill requiring every agent for a corporation that accepts money for products and services to provide a physical address. That way we can track down scoundrels and ring their necks!

***

It's bad enough that some people don't dot their i's and cross their t's. But people who don't even bother to make their i's or t's at all, well… they are a whole other sort.

***

A guy infuriated me the other day. I didn't think telling him to "go jump in the lake" was strong enough. So I said, "Go jump in a lake and stay at the bottom."

***

When someone says, "Every day you get out of bed is a good day," you know he's having a bad day.

104

You know a friend is losing his patience with someone when he says, "I don't let that guy bother me one bit."

***

John fourteen-two. One day I'll be looking down from a mansion, and in the glow, it will be as if I were looking down from an airplane at the tragedies we faced in life. They will appear as small and insignificant as rats running across a brown field.

***

If you nourish them, roses can grow roots in the ashes of tragedy.

***

If your new baby is laughing before you start singing, and his face sours after a few bars, you definitely can't sing.

***

A guy with no top covering asked me, "What's the best thing about having all your hair fall out?"
"I don't know," I replied.
He said, "You don't have to worry about your hair falling out."

***

My wife told me I was snoring so loud that even if she were Helen Keller, she'd still have slept in the guest bedroom.

***

"If your wife makes an unwelcomed comment to you, do not answer back. These words would be the first sentence of the next argument." Anonymous

If you wake up from a mad dream, be grateful you are able to experience your share of trauma with the ability to forget about it quickly.

After writing a large check to pay my taxes, my distress was eased by music from the Baroque period playing on the radio.

***

Bizarre, painful situations are the vat in which the frothiest humor is brewed.

***

There is a fine line between achieving the patience of a saint and being a glutton for punishment!

***

Sometimes you have to let go to hold on.

***

Some people give up their faith in God because of the awful things that happen in the world. I'm not letting Him off the hook that easily. I've kept a diary of my gripes. I'm going to request a seat on the interrogation committee that poses to Him the tough questions when we meet in the hereafter.

***

From what I can see, most people plead for material possessions, love, and good health. And what's wrong with that? But true peace of mind will come when you pray for, and achieve, the patience, stamina, and courage to endure the insanity until it finds someone else to haunt. Then the struggle pays off because we have earned the stripes that enable us to give comfort to someone else.

Life is the strangest thing that's ever happened to me.

***

Listening to melancholy music can be like getting sore muscles massaged.

***

We all get to our wit's end sometimes and vow to ourselves, "That's it!" We imagine carrying out plans to escape the madness. But sometimes the only thing we can do is to grow a longer wit.

A Nightcap of Fiction

The Stockton Diet

Chip Stockton could not get to sleep no matter what he tried. Counting backwards from one hundred proved futile. Picturing himself on a beach in the Bahamas in a state of complete relaxation was not helping. He was hungry. He could not deny it. Powerful hungry. Hot air blew up from the heating grate and annoyed the curtains. The vision of peanut butter slathered on a slice of bread danced in his head. It just might carry him until breakfast.

For the last couple of weeks he had been enduring misery in his quest to reduce. Soon he would have his twentieth class reunion, and feared his old buddies would tease him about the potbelly he had amassed over the years. He had gotten so rotund he could not see over this mound when he lay on the beach.

He told himself "No," but his body was saying, "Yes" as he found himself rising from his bed. He moved ever so gently so as not to wake Eloise, who was snoring lightly. He slid his feet into his slippers, and lifted his robe off its hook. He put his arms through the sleeves and tied it at his waist, which seemed to have shrunk an appreciable amount. He tiptoed down the stairs, salivating.

In the kitchen, he found some rice cakes in the cabinet where the peanut butter was usually stored. How could anyone consider them food? When he opened the fridge, his heart dropped to the floor. It all came back to him. Despite her initial protest, Eloise had given in to Chip's appeal to remove all foods from the house that evening, except those considered "diet." He scrutinized the fridge and saw nothing but raw baby carrots, celery sticks, and broccoli, yogurt, a jar of salsa, low fat mayo, and some browned tuna fish in a plastic container. No mayo. Eight friggin bottles of seltzer water.

He had tried Weight Watchers, Nutrisystems, Atkins, Slimfast. He had tried the not-so-famous schemes. Strong's Low Carb Diet, Barbarossa's High Protein. The Stuff Yourself Once-A-Week Plan. But after a few stressful days strung together like sausages, he would find himself in the kitchen after work cramming his mouth with leftovers.

But now, there was nothing anyone would consider food in the house. He hated Eloise for clearing the fridge—even if he had commanded her to do so.

His put the wheels of his mind in motion. It was two a.m. The fast food hamburger and taco joints in town closed at midnight. Even Pat's Hubba Hubba, which made the best pizza burgers anywhere, would have shut off the grill by this time.

A lovely, vivid image of the Champion Diner, an all-night joint, shined in his mind. Yes! Yes! Their hamburger platter didn't come with Five Guys seasoned fries, but it was good and filling. Even the dinner salad, with crunchy chicken and chunky blue cheese dressing might do. Realizing Jack Kraustenhauer would be on night duty as the manager doused his plans. He feared Eloise might find out if he cheated. She often went into the diner for coffee with girlfriends, and Jack and the other guys would spill the beans to her and tell jokes about his struggle. Boy, could he go for a can of Bush's baked beans—maple and brown sugar type.

An idea so ingenious came into his mind that he tried to understand how he had generated it. He concluded it had magnificently popped up from his subconscious. He was like one of the great poets who claimed their greatest ideas came out of the blue. No matter, hope leapt in his heart, and he began to feel warm and fuzzy all over. He salivated and sucked up the juices.

He pulled the slider open, and found himself standing on the back deck on a chilly fall early morning. All was dark, still, and quiet. Dry leaves lay scattered on the back lawn, and he walked gingerly so as not to make crunching noises.

The temperature had been nice and cool since the early afternoon. Certainly enough that food left outside would not have spoiled. He realized their teenage son Artie, and eight-year-old Amy, would ridicule him to no end if they caught him. Eloise would really scorn him.

But he was so crazed he could not hold himself back. He tiptoed over towards the garage. He couldn't believe he was going to do it, but what could be *morally* wrong with such an action? And he could sympathize with himself. What else could a ravenous man do in his situation?

Chip Stockton lifted the lid off the garbage pail, and a raccoon appeared a short distance away to greet him. At least this guy didn't spray like the skunk that had dug a home under the family shed. Chip shooed the small harmless beast away with his foot. "Get out of here. Go on, get," he whispered louder than he should have. The creature disappeared into the night.

He felt angry when he found creamed corn splashed over everything. Bad enough the kids left it on their plates when he had craved more at the dinner table. Oh well... He lifted the plastic shopping bags and laid them on the ground. The first one yielded only spoiling vegetables. Eloise always bought too much salad and too many cukes, forgetting she had stowed them in the crisper drawer.

In the next bag, he hit pay dirt. It was as if Eloise had a premonition and had packed the leftovers for him. Maybe it was out of the kindness of her subconscious. In reclosable Baggies, he found Tuesday's sloppy Joes, Wednesday's chicken parm and pasta, and the pot roast and mashed potatoes of the night before. Sweet Eloise.

Chip ripped open the pot roast bag, tore off a hunk, and rubbed it in the mashed. Delight shot through his entire being as he shoved it in his mouth and chewed. What savory meat Eloise created! Good cold as warm. After polishing it off, he stuck his fingers in the sloppy Joes and fed his mouth maniacally. Who could season it better than the little lady? Next came the chicken parm. How did Eloise get the chicken so tender it melted in your mouth? Sensational. Then the lasagna, always better the next day.

He had remained loyal to the diet for a couple of weeks now, so a night of chowing down could do no lasting harm. In fact, this meal fit synergistically with the "Stuff Yourself One Day a Week Diet."

The fires of stress and strain were being extinguished this glorious autumn evening. In the cool, crisp air, he gazed upward, and was darned if he couldn't see the lips of the man in the moon curve into a smile. Was that crumbled blue cheese all over his face?

The rascal appeared again from the corner of the garage. Why couldn't he dine in peace? Chip threw the spoiling vegetables to keep the raccoon occupied, but as he did, he bumped the garbage pail. The metal lid fell to the ground, and created an awful clanging noise.

Chip was startled when his next-door neighbor Clifford Baltry threw up his sash and hollered. "Hey! Who's there? What are you doing in that yard?"

Remaining silent, Chip stood there, marinating in shame. But it was too dark for Baltry to recognize him.

"Get out of that yard, or I'll call the cops!"

Chip ran towards his sliding glass door in his slippers, but tripped and tumbled to the ground. The back floodlight came on. By the time he got up and scrambled onward, the kitchen ceiling was illuminated, and spotlights shone on the backyard.

Eloise appeared on the deck. She walked within several feet of him. He could feel the weight of her stare taking a picture of him. She scowled, and Chip felt like a little boy being chastised by his mother again. He examined his hands and saw they were covered with the mashed potatoes and sloppy Joe sauce.

Soon Baltry, tall and gangly as ever, appeared, breathing heavily from his dash. He asked the Stocktons if all was okay. "I saw an intruder by your garage." He paused, and he too, noticed Chip's hand, as well as the food residue on his face. "Was that you at the trash pail, Stockton?" Baltry grinned.

"What's with all that food on your face?" Eloise's eyebrows furrowed.

He would have punched Baltry in the face the way the wise guy gawked at him, but not with his family present. "Why don't you go home and get your beauty sleep, Baltry?"

"Daddy, you have food all over your face." Little Amy's expression was more inquisitive than scolding.

Everyone turned with Eloise, and light shone on the trash pail and the food bags beside it.

"Were you eating out of the trash, Stockton?" Baltry had some audacity.

"You're trespassing Baltry," Chip barked.

What can I say? Chip asked himself. But he blurted out, "Let me explain... It's not what it looks like..."

113

Amy crossed her arms at her chest and grinned. "Daddy, don't even try. You're so busted!"

Eloise closed her robe more tightly at her chest. She shook her head, grimaced, and walked inside.

www.sthaggerty.com

S.T. Haggerty served as a magazine editor at McGraw-Hill Publications in New York. As a freelance writer, he has published articles in a variety of newspapers and magazines. He began his journalism career as a college senior, writing sports articles for the Bennington Banner in Vermont.

He also conducted interviews about rural farm life with some of the locals from his village in Vermont. Material from Haggerty's interviews appeared in *The Yellow Farmhouse Cookbook,* and *Dear Charlie,* both by Christopher Kimball, who is editor and publisher of "Cook's Illustrated" magazine, and host of the television program, "America's Test Kitchen" as seen on The Food Network.

He received his master's degree in Journalism from the University of South Carolina where he attended on a scholarship, and was assistant to the director of the S.C.S.P.A., the state's high school press association. His concentration was in creative fiction and non-fiction. He placed third in USC's fiction writing contest.

From Southern Vermont College, he earned his B.S. degree magna cum laude in business/communications with a minor in English Literature.

He is an alumnus of the American Society of Magazine Editors Internship Program, and was chosen as one of three American students by the vice president of McGraw-Hill as an editorial trainee. He was mentored by Jan Tuchman, currently the editor-in-chief of *Engineering News-Record,* the country's leading construction magazine.

Among his teachers have been B.K. Fischer, Poetry Editor of the *Boston Review*; William Emerson Jr., former editor-in-chief of the original *Saturday Evening Post*; William Price Fox, novelist and writer-in-residence at the University of South Carolina: and Madeleine L'Engle, novelist and poet, who wrote the Newbury Medal-winning novel, *A Wrinkle in Time.*

S.T. Haggerty is a member of the Mahopac Writer's Group led by author and popular speaker, Vinny Dacquino.

He is currently employed as a project manager on construction job sites. A master painter and carpenter, he also teaches these trades.

Made in the USA
Middletown, DE
19 January 2023